Bible Colouring
&
Activity Sheets

-

The Book
of
Genesis

A photocopiable resource

Created and
illustrated
by
Jo Maslen

Table of Contents

The BEGINNING of the WORLD

Read the story in Genesis chapter 1

Draw some more animals in the spaces

Find these words in the Grid

Beginning	Stars	Rested
Day	Sun	God
Water	Moon	Sea
Sky	Fish	Night
Heaven	Birds	Spirit
Earth	Animals	Seasons
Trees	Adam	Light
Land	Eve	Dark

Word Search Grid:

```
W  B S T E F I S H H C S D R I B
O  H E A V E N O O M K S L W D N
R  U E G O D A E S R R G I A O K
D  H R F I D R A A K B Y T M R
S  V T L A N D T A S K R E V E
E  M G Y W J N S H S B F R P S
A  A N I G H T I U C S P I R I T
R  C D A S E A S O N S T H G I L E
C  H A N I M A L S D G E N A M N D
```

Hold the page to a mirror to find the

MEMORY VERSE

AND GOD SAW ALL
THAT HE HAD MADE,
AND IT WAS VERY GOOD
GENESIS ch 1 v 31

| Day 1 | Day 2 | Day 3 | Day 4 | Day 5 | Day 6 | Day 7 |

Draw a picture to show what was made on each day of creation

ADAM and EVE

Draw a picture of Eve being made from Adam

MEMORY VERSE - GENESIS ch 1 v 27   So God created man in his own image

QUESTIONS

1. On which day were Adam & Eve made?

2. How many rivers were in the garden of Eden?

3. Which tree were they not allowed to eat from?

4. Who named all the animals?

5. How was Eve made?

Write your answers to these questions here

ANSWERS

1.

2.

3.

4.

5.

Take the first letter of each object to find one of the rivers in the garden

 THE FALL

FOR ALL HAVE SINNED AND FALL SHORT OF THE GLORY OF GOD
ROMANS CH 3 V 23

Answer the questions to find out where the tree was in the garden
(All the answers are in Genesis ch 3)

Who listened to his wife? v 17

What weren't they allowed to eat from the tree? v 3

What was the fruit desirable for gaining? v 6

What was Eden? v 24

What did the serpent have to crawl on? v 14

What did they do to the fig leaves? v 7

Draw the serpent talking to Eve

CAIN AND ABEL

Read the story in Genesis chapter 4

Draw Cain working in the field

Draw Abel looking after his sheep

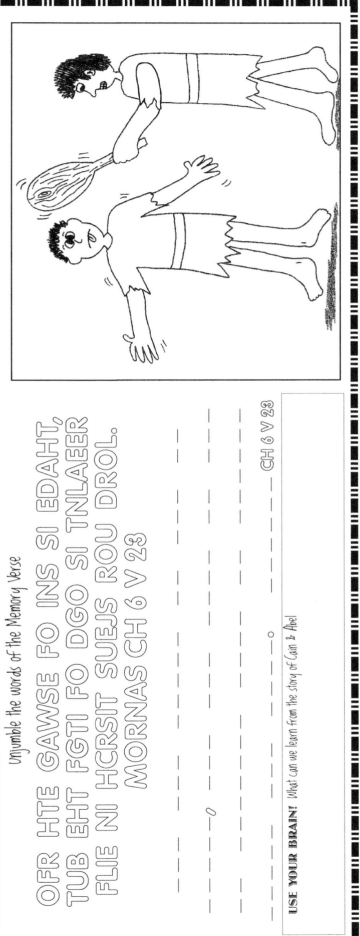

Unjumble the words of the Memory Verse

OFR HTE GAWSE FO INS SI EDAHT,
TUB EHT FGTI FO DGO SI TNLAEER
FLIE NI HCRSIT SUEJS ROU DROL.
MORNAS CH 6 V 23

_ _ _   _ _ _   _ _ _ _ _   _ _   _ _ _   _ _   _ _ _ _ _,

_ _ _   _ _ _   _ _ _ _   _ _   _ _ _   _ _   _ _ _ _ _ _ _

_ _ _ _   _ _   _ _ _ _ _ _   _ _ _ _ _   _ _ _   _ _ _ _.

CH 6 V 23

USE YOUR BRAIN! What can we learn from the story of Cain & Abel

ADAM - NOAH

Read the story in Genesis chapter 5

Fill in the gaps on the Family Tree

Crack the code to find the Memory Verse

A	B	C	D	E	F	G	H	I	J	K	L	M
Z	Y	X	W	V	U	T	S	R	Q	P	O	N

N	O	P	Q	R	S	T	U	V	W	X	Y	Z
M	L	K	J	I	H	G	F	E	D	C	B	A

VMLXS DZOPVW DRGS TLW

TVMVHRH CH 5 V 24

_ _ _ _ _ _ _ _ _

_ _ _ _ _ _ _ _ _

_ _ _ _ _ _ _ _ _

CH 5 V 24

Family Tree

ADAM
↓
- - - -
↓
ENOSH
↓
- - - -
↓
MAHALALEL
↓
- - - -
↓
ENOCH →
↓
- - - -
↓
LAMECH
↓
- - - -

This family tree covered about 2000 years

QUESTION TIME

1. How old was Enoch when he became the father of Methuselah?

2. For how many years did Enoch walk with God?

3. Methuselah was the oldest man in the Bible, how old was he when he died?

4. How many years did Enoch live?

5. What happened to Enoch?

Colour this picture of Enoch talking to God

HOW MANY WORDS CAN YOU MAKE FROM METHUSELAH? WRITE YOUR WORDS ON THE BACK OF THIS SHEET

THE FLOOD

(PART 1)

You can read the story for yourself in Genesis chapter 6

NOAH PREPARES THE ARK

Draw a picture of Noah, his wife, his 3 sons & their wives

Find these words in the grid

N	D	G	I	L	W	A
B	O	C	A	N	I	D
D	O	A	P	R	C	R
C	L	E	H	N	K	U
R	F	L	I	F	E	A
E	J	G	W	O	D	N
A	V	T	W	M	N	I
T	H	T	R	A	E	M
U	C	F	A	H	S	A
R	T	S	I	S	S	L
E	I	Q	N	S	H	R
S	P	O	K	H	E	O
O	S	C	M	K	M	O
P	E	R	I	S	H	F
D	E	V	E	I	R	G

Noah
God
Wickedness
Earth
Grieved
Pitch
Flood
Ark
Roof
Decks

Life
Creatures
Rain
Two
Sons
Animal
Shem
Ham
in
Perish

Crack the Code to find the Memory Verse

a = x	f = s	k = o	p = i
b = w	g = r	l = n	q = e
c = v	h = q	m = l	r = g
d = u	i = m	n = k	s = f
e = t	j = p	o = j	t = h

u = c
v = a
w = d
x = b
y = z   z = y

lkvt wpw qcqgzetplr odfe vf Rkw ukiivlwqw tpi

___ ___ ___ _____ ____ __ ___ _____ ___

Genesis chapter 6 v 22

THE FLOOD (PART 2)

Read the story for yourself in Genesis chapter 7 – 8 v 5

MEMORY VERSE

...and Noah did all that the LORD commanded him. Genesis ch 7 v 5

THE ANIMALS ENTER THE ARK

Draw pairs of animals going into the ark

Think of the name of the animal's partner & write them in the spaces

ANIMAL	MALE	FEMALE
Sheep	Ram	
Horse		Mare
Elephant	Bull	
Pig		Sow

ANIMAL	MALE	FEMALE
Rabbit	Buck	
Chicken		Hen
Whale		
Duck	Drake	Cow

THE FLOOD (PART 3)

Read the story for yourself in
Genesis chapter 8 v 5 – 9 v 17

MEMORY VERSE – Genesis ch 9 v 11 Never again will all life be cut off by the waters of a flood.

Answer the questions to
find the sign of the promise

What will fall on all the animals?
Genesis ch 9 v 2

Genesis ch 8 v 6

Genesis ch 9 v 2

Genesis ch 9 v 11

Genesis ch 9 v 10

What kind of leaf?
Genesis ch 8 v 12

Genesis ch 9 v 2

Come out of where?

All of which creatures?

When would the Earth be flooded again?

Which kind of flying creatures?

Genesis ch 8 v 11

What did Noah do for the next 7 days?

THE SONS OF NOAH

You can read all about them in Genesis chapter 9

Unjumble the words to find the Memory Verse in Numbers ch 32 v 23

...OYU YMA EB ESRU TTAH OYRU NSI LHLI DFNI OYU UTO.

_ _ _   _ _ _   _ _   _ _ _ _

_ _ _ _   _ _ _ _ _   _ _ _   _ _ _ _

_ _ _ _   _ _ _   _ _ _ .

Draw your own picture of Ham, Shem and Japheth

Find the words of the Memory Verse in the Grid

A	K	P	L	S	E	B	Y
F	S	L	Y	U	I	C	O
W	I	U	H	C	T	A	U
W	N	N	R	O	H	Y	B
R	H	E	D	E	A	O	G
O	M	F	K	M	T	U	L
U	I	R	G	L	O	R	W
Y	N	P	D	S	D	O	T
B	T	K	T	U	O	Z	M
N	W	V	U	R	X	E	F

how many words can you make from HAM, SHEM & JAPHETH write them on the back of your sheet

Draw the men building the Tower of Babel

fill in the missing words

v6 The Lord said, "If as one people .... the same .... they have begun to do this then nothing they .... to do will be .... for them.

v7 Come, let us .... down and .... their language so they will not .... each other"

v8 So the .... scattered them from there over the whole .... and they stopped .... the city

v9 That is .... it was called ...., because there the Lord .... the language of the .... world.

Draw lines from the squares to the circles to match the greeting with the language

(Hello)   [German]   (Boreda)

[French]   [Spanish]

(Hola)   (Gutentag)

[Welsh]

(Bonjour)   [English]

THE TOWER OF BABEL

MEMORY VERSE

'Set your mind on things above, not on earthly things.'
Colossians ch 3 v 2

God speaks to Abram

Read the story in Genesis ch 12

"I will make you into a great _ _ _ _ _ _ and I will _ _ _ _ _ _ you; I will make your _ _ _ _ great and you will be a _ _ _ _ _ _ _ _ . I will _ _ _ _ _ those who _ _ _ _ _ you, and whoever _ _ _ _ _ _ you, I will _ _ _ _ _; all peoples on _ _ _ _ _ will be _ _ _ _ _ _ _ through you."

Genesis ch 12 v 1

Draw Abram leaving Haran with Sarai, Lot, his possessions, and all the other people

Answer the Questions:

1. Why did Abram go to Egypt to live?

2. Why did Abram tell Sarai to lie to Pharaoh?

3. How did pharaoh treat Abram when he thought Sarai was his sister?

4. What did Pharaoh give Abram?

5. What happened to Pharaoh as a result of Abram's lie?

6. What did Pharaoh then do to Abram?

MEMORY VERSE

"...keep your tongue from evil and your lips from speaking lies"
Psalm 34 v 13

ABRAM and LOT - Read the story in GENESIS chapters 13 and 14

Answer the questions to find out where Abram started from

Where did he put his tent? ch 13 v 3

From Egypt Abram went through where? ch 13 v 3

For 12 what were they subject to Kedorlaomer? ch 14 v 4

What relation was Lot to Abram? ch 14 v 12

What pit did the men fall into? ch 14 v 10

Where did Abram start from?

Draw Lot going east and Abram going west

Hold the page up to a mirror to
find the MEMORY VERSE

Ephesians ch 5 v 8

for ye were by grace you
have been saved
through faith
and that not of
yourselves
it is the gift of God

*Unjumble the letters to
find where Lot &
Abram went*

OMSDO

NAACAN

How many words can you make from the defeated king's name? **KEDORLAOMER** Write your words on the back of your sheet

God's promise to Abraham

Read this story in Genesis ch 15

Memory Verse - The Lord said this to Abram & He says the same thing to YOU today!

"Do not be afraid _____. (Write your name)
I am your shield, your very great reward"

Genesis ch 15 v 1

find these words in the grid

C	H	I	L	D	R	E	N	A	R	B
O	C	S	E	V	A	L	S	E	N	L
U	N	E	S	N	U	S	F	N	O	O
N	P	H	R	M	R	I	O	R	I	R
T	O	C	A	A	E	E	D	G	S	A
M	A	R	T	H	G	M	O	H	I	E
I	B	O	S	I	V	A	V	A	V	Y
A	S	T	P	I	T	P	E	E	L	S

Lord   ram
Abram   dove
vision   pigeon
no   deep
children   sleep
count   torch
stars   slaves
heifer   year
goat   sun

Hagar & Ishmael

Read this story in Genesis ch 16

What did the Lord say to Hagar? Use your Bible to fill in the gaps:

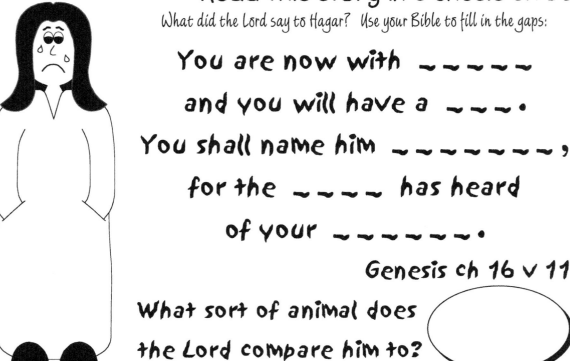

You are now with _ _ _ _ _ _

and you will have a _ _ _ _.

You shall name him _ _ _ _ _ _ _ _,

for the _ _ _ _ _ has heard

of your _ _ _ _ _ _ _ _.

Genesis ch 16 v 11

What sort of animal does
the Lord compare him to?

SODOM AND GOMORRAH

Read the story in Genesis chs 18 and 19

Draw a picture of Abraham pleading with God for the city of Sodom

Answer the Questions from chapter 19

What did Lot do when he saw the two angels? (v1)

What did the men tell Lot that God had told them to do? (v13)

What time of day was it when the angels told Lot to get out of the city? (v15)

What instructions did the angels give Lot after leading them out of the city? (v17)

What happened to Lot's wife as a consequence of looking back? (v26)

In which town did Lot & his daughters stay for a short time? (v30)

MEMORY VERSE

"For it is by grace you have been saved, through faith- and this not from yourselves, it is the gift of God not by works, so that no one can boast"

EPHESIANS ch 2 v 8 and 9

FIND THE WORDS OF THE MEMORY VERSE

B	C	U	G	Y	O	U	R	S	E	L	V	F	E
O	F	O	R	M	C	A	N	B	Y	D	E	A	T
A	N	Y	A	O	T	D	F	Y	O	D	F	I	H
S	A	B	C	R	H	S	G	G	M	N	O	T	A
T	A	P	E	F	I	T	H	R	O	U	G	H	T
O	B	V	H	E	S	W	O	R	K	S	O	O	F
R	A	S	E	B	N	O	T	T	H	E	L	N	O
H	V	N	A	D	L	O	H	G	I	F	T	E	S
T	W	Y	D	S	E	V	L	E	S	R	U	O	Y
U	E	P	H	E	S	I	A	N	S	S	T	U	Y

How many words can you make from

SODOM AND GOMORRAH

Write your words on the back of your sheet

ABRAHAM & ABIMELECH

You can find this story in Genesis Ch 20

Draw the story in cartoons

Abimelech with Abraham and Sarah	God speaking to Abimelech through his dream	Abimelech giving Abraham sheep, cattle & slaves

Unjumble the jumbled words to find the Memory Verse:

"**heT drLo** detests **ylign sipl, ubt eH** delights **ni emn**
(or children) **owh rea** truthful"   Proverbs 12 v 22

"_ _ _ _ _ _ _ detests _ _ _ _ _ _ _ _ _, _ _ _ _ _

delights _ _ _ _ _ (or children) _ _ _ _ _ _ truthful"
Proverbs 12 v 22

ISAAC IS BORN

You can find this story in Genesis Ch 21 V 1-7

What had God promised Abraham & Sarah? (v2)

How old was Isaac when he was circumcised? (v4)

How old was Abraham when Isaac was born? (v5)

What does the name Isaac mean? Solve the clues to find out:

2nd letter of	6th letter of	2nd letter of	3rd letter of	4th letter of	2nd letter of	2nd letter of	3rd letter of

Hagar and Ishmael

You can read the story in Genesis ch 21 v 8 - 21

Have you ever been in a situation where you felt lonely like Hagar?

How did it make you feel?

Do you know anyone who's lonely?

How can you help them?

Solve the clues to find out which desert Hagar wandered in.

Draw Sarah telling Abraham to get rid of Hagar

" __ __ __ __
__ __ __ , __ __
__ __ __ __
Psalm 46 v 1

Who held a great feast? (v8)

What was Ishmael going to be? (v18)

What was in the skin? (v14)

In which desert was Ishmael when he got married? (v21)

Under what did Hagar put Ishmael? (v15)

What did Ishmael become in the desert? (v20)

Where did the angel of God call from? (v17)

What did Hagar begin to do? (v16)

What nationality was Hagar? (v9)

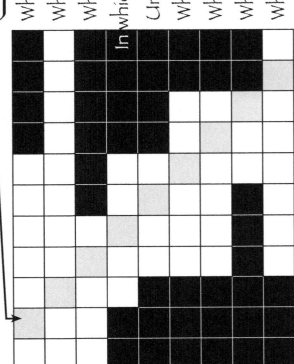

ABRAHAM TESTED

You can read the story in Genesis ch 22 v 1 - 19

Who spoke to Abraham? (v 2)

What time of day did they set off? (v 3)

What did Isaac ask Abraham? (v 7)

What did Abraham build? (v9)

What did Abraham call the place where the ram was caught in the thicket? (v 14)

Draw the ram stuck in the bush

When you have found all the words in the grid, you should have 6 letters left which make up the name of the mountain where all this happened!

H	M	S	B	U	R	N	T
A	N	T	K	O	I	E	S
N	E	A	R	Y	S	O	N
D	V	R	I	T	A	C	R
A	A	S	E	K	A	D	O
O	E	D	N	U	C	R	H
F	H	I	G	Y	T	O	D
F	F	H	A	H	R	L	B
E	T	L	I	A	Y	M	S
R	F	R	M	E	A	E	D
I	D	I	K	L	R	T	E
N	O	N	R	V	R	E	D
G	O	D	A	E	L	K	I
D	W	N	H	B	E	C	V
D	T	T	L	O	G	I	O
S	A	O	O	Y	N	H	R
F	W	Y	H	N	A	T	P
T	M	A	H	A	R	B	A

God	knife
tested	ram
Abraham	caught
Isaac	horns
only	thicket
son	Lord
donkey	provided
wood	do
burnt	not
offering	lay
two	hand
servants	boy
third	angel
day	heaven
father	stars
fire	sky
lamb	

"By faith Abraham, when God tested him, offered Isaac as a sacrifice"

Hebrews ch 11 v 17

ISAAC and REBEKAH

You can read this story in *Genesis ch 24*

Draw pictures to re-tell the story

Abraham talking to his servant

Rebekah giving Abraham's servant a drink

Abraham's servant talking to Laban

Rebekah seeing Isaac for the first time

How many words can you make from **ISAAC AND REBEKAH**
Write your words on the back of your sheet

How do you think you'd feel if your dad sent someone to find you a husband or wife?

Take the first letter of each object to find out the name of Rebekah's dad

Hold your sheet to a mirror to find the Memory Verse:

Trust in the Lord with all your heart and lean not on your own understanding. Proverbs ch 3 v 5

JACOB & ESAU

You can read the story in Genesis ch 25 v 19 - 34

Jacob& Esau

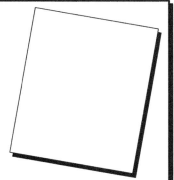

Write the story of the Jacob and Esau using your own words and pictures

How old was Isaac when he married Rebekah? (v20)

What colour was Esau when he was born? (v25)

What was Jacob holding when he was born? (v26)

How old was Isaac when the twins were born? (v26)

What did Esau like doing? (v27)

Which of the twins did Isaac like best? (v28)

What did Esau want from Jacob? (v30)

What did Jacob want from Esau? (v31)

Memory Verse

"²⁰By faith Isaac blessed Jacob and Esau in regard to their future"

Hebrews ch 11 v 20

JACOB IS BLESSED BY ISAAC, THEN RUNS AWAY FROM ESAU

You can read the story in Genesis ch 27 & 28

Fill in the gaps to find the Memory Verse

"I _ _ _ with _ _ and _ _ _ _ _ watch _ _ _ you wherever

_ _ _ go, and I _ _ _ _ bring you _ _ _ _ to this _ _ _ _

I will _ _ _ _ leave you _ _ _ _ I have _ _ _ _ what I

_ _ _ _ _ _ _ you"

Genesis ch 28 v 15

DRAW JACOB SLEEPING & DREAMING

Find the words below in the grid

R	W	O	M	E	N	A	B	E	R	D	A	P
E	I	H	A	R	A	N	E	D	N	I	F	A
B	S	H	N	A	L	L	I	K	R	S	E	D
E	H	M	G	I	F	H	S	S	E	P	T	A
K	M	A	R	A	J	T	A	C	H	L	I	N
A	A	J	Y	A	N	A	A	C	T	E	N	M
H	E	O	U	A	B	L	C	J	O	A	A	A
O	L	A	B	S	E	A	P	O	R	S	A	R
H	S	A	M	A	N	H	A	S	B	I	N	A
E	L	S	E	H	E	A	P	H	R	N	A	A
E	F	I	W	J	N	M	E	B	M	G	C	I

Esau
kill
Jacob
Rebekah
flee
brother
Laban

Haran
angry
Isaac
find
wife
Padan
Aram

Cananite
women
displeasing
Ishmael
Mahalath

Unjumble the words
(use the clues if you get stuck)
All the clues are found in Genesis ch 27

SAIAC _____ Who had weak eyes? (v 1)

HKEERBA _____ Who was listening to Isaac? (v 5)

RIAHY _____ What sort of man was Esau? (v 11)

MOSOHT _____ What sort of skin did Jacob have? (v 11)

INWE _____ What did Jacob give Isaac to drink? (v 25)

CBJOA _____ Whose voice did Isaac hear? (v 22)

NNTIAOS _____ Who will serve Jacob? (v29)

DERTLEMB _____ What did Isaac do violently? (v 33)

PWTE _____ What did Esau do aloud? (v 38)

Jacob gets married and has children
You can read this story in Genesis chapters 29 and 30

Where did the shepherds come from? (v4)

Who was Nahor's grandson? (v5)

What was Rachel's job? (v9)

What did Jacob do after he'd watered the sheep? (v11)

Who was Jacob's mum? (v12)

What did Jacob want in return for seven years work? (v18)

Who did Jacob actually marry? (v23)

For how many more years did Jacob have to work to get Rachel as his wife? (v27)

> Jacob was willing to wait 14 years so he could marry Rachel.
> He had lots of patience!
> Patience is one of the fruits of the Spirit (or qualities of a Christian).
> Look up in your Bible Galatians chapter 5 verse 22 to find the other fruits & write them here:

MEMORY VERSE
"COMMIT TO THE LORD WHATEVER YOU DO, AND YOUR PLANS WILL SUCCEED"
PROVERBS CH 16 V 3

Draw pictures of Jacob's children
(The name of their mum is in brackets)

Reuben (Leah)	Simeon (Leah)	Levi (Leah)	Judah (Leah)	Dan (Bilhah)	Naphtali (Bilhah)
1	**2**	**3**	**4**	**5**	**6**
Gad (Zilpah)	Asher (Zilpah)	Issachar (Leah)	Zebulun (Leah)	Dinah (Leah)	Joseph (Rachel)
7	**8**	**9**	**10**	**11**	**12**

JACOB and LABAN

You can read this story in Genesis ch 30 v 25 - ch 31 v 55

Memory Verse

"WITHOUT FAITH IT IS IMPOSSIBLE TO PLEASE GOD"

HEBREWS CH 11 v 6

IT'S QUESTION TIME!

All the answers can be found in chapter 31

Where did the Lord tell Jacob to go? (v3)

What animal did Rachel & Leah ride? (v17)

Where did Jacobs father Isaac live? (v18)

What did Rachel steal from her father? (v19)

How long had Jacob worked for Laban? (v38)

What did Laban want to make with Jacob? (v44)

In whose name did Jacob take an oath? (v53)

Jacob had to run away from Laban – in your own words write the story of how Jacob got all the strong & healthy sheep on the back of your sheet

Colour Jacob's sheep blue and Laban's sheep red!

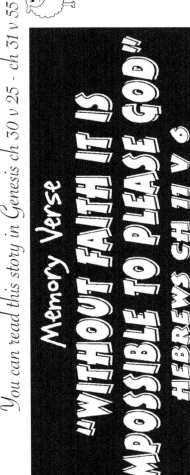
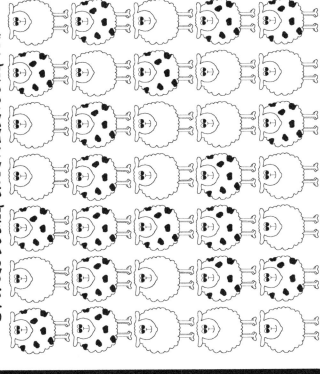

Jacob wrestles with God

You can read this story in Genesis ch 32

Jacob wanted to give Esau some of his animals as a gift, how many of each animal did he give?

Female goats

Male goats

Ewes

Rams

Female donkeys

Male donkeys

Female camels & their young

Cows

Bulls

Memory Verse

"The LORD is good, a refuge in times of trouble. He cares for those who trust in Him."

Nahum chapter 1 verse 7

Find the words below in the grid

T	S	J	D	E	H	C	N	E	R	W
E	O	D	L	T	A	D	C	O	P	I
Y	C	E	E	E	K	E	O	I	S	V
L	K	R	A	N	O	L	H	G	N	E
I	E	A	R	D	B	T	S	N	O	S
F	T	P	S	O	B	S	M	E	I	M
E	B	S	I	N	A	E	M	G	S	O
A	B	O	C	A	J	R	A	N	S	R
N	M	A	N	F	S	W	E	I	E	N
E	D	E	A	S	U	V	R	P	S	I
M	S	C	E	A	E	B	T	M	S	N
A	E	L	T	L	O	R	S	I	O	G
N	B	P	E	N	I	E	L	L	P	H

Jacob	morning	God
wives	socket	face
eleven	hip	yet
sons	wrenched	life
Jabbok	bless	spared
stream	me	limping
possessions	name	tendon
man	Israel	
wrestled	Peniel	

Jacob meets Esau

You can read this story in Genesis chapter 33

Draw Esau running to meet Jacob

Unjumble the letters to find the Memory Verse

"keMa ersu ttha dyobon ysap
kbca gornw orf gornw, ubt swaya
yrt ot eb dkni ot heac rtohe ......"

1 Thessalonians ch 5 v 15

How many words can you make from
JACOB AND ESAU?
Write your words on
the back of your sheet

How many men were with Esau when he met Jacob? Use the clues below to find out:

| 4th letter of | 3rd letter of | 1st letter of | 4th letter of | 4th letter of | 2nd letter of | 6th letter of | 4th letter of | 4th letter of | 4th letter of | 2nd letter of | 4th letter of |

Jacob returns to Bethel

You can read about Jacob's return in Genesis chapter 35

Follow the arrows to tell the story of Jacob's return to Canaan:

Where did God tell Jacob to go? (v1) B _ _ _ _ _ _

Draw Jacob building an altar

What did he have to build? (v1) A _ _ _ _ _

What did Jacob tell his household to get rid of? (v2)
F _ _ _ _ _ _ _   g _ _ _

What sort of things could be like gods in our lives?
(Things that take our attention away from God)

Who died? (v8)
D _ _ _ _ _ _ _

Who appeared to Jacob? (v9) G _ _   What did Jacob's name change to? (v10) I _ _ _ _ _ _

Draw Jacob setting it up

What did Jacob set up? (v14) S _ _ _ _ _   P _ _ _ _ _ _

Who died? (v19)
R _ _ _ _ _ _

Who was born? (v18)
B _ _ _ _ _ _ _ _

Who died? (v29)
I _ _ _ _ _

How old was he when he died? (v28)

MEMORY VERSE

"Surely God is my salvation;
I will trust and not be afraid"
Isaiah chapter 12 verse 2

Joseph dreams & is sold by his brothers

You can read this story in Genesis chapter 37

Draw pictures to retell the story of Joseph's dreaming

Joseph in his coat of many colours	Sheaves of corn dream	Sun, moon and stars dream	Jacob telling Joseph off

Colour in the boxes with a dot to find the memory verse

D	R	Y	O	U	W	O	K	N	O	W	D	O	N	E	W	I	T	H	A	L	L	A	L	L
B	Y	O	U	R	T	H	E	A	R	T	G	O	D	A	N	D	T	H	A	T	S	O	U	L
T	H	A	T	E	N	O	T	H	R	O	N	E	A	R	O	F	W	A	L	L	A	T	H	E
B	E	G	O	O	D	O	N	I	P	R	O	M	I	S	E	S	A	M	O	T	H	E	R	S
L	O	R	D	A	Y	O	U	R	U	N	G	O	D	B	I	G	A	V	E	Y	E	Y	O	U
P	H	A	S	E	F	A	I	L	E	D	O	J	O	S	H	U	A	C	H	2	3	V	1	4

ANSWER THE QUESTIONS

Where did Joseph find his brothers? (v17)

Who stopped Joseph from being killed? (v21)

Who did the brothers sell Joseph to? (v27)

What animal did the brothers kill? (v31)

JOSEPH & POTIPHAR'S WIFE

You can read this story in Genesis chapter 39

QUESTIONS!

In which country was Joseph living? (v1)

What did Joseph look like? (v6)

What did Potiphar's wife want Joseph to do? (v7)

What did Joseph's do? (v10)

What did Joseph leave with Potiphar's wife? (v13)

What did Potiphar do when he heard his wife's side of the story? (v20)

What did the Lord show Joseph while he was in prison? (v21)

What did the prison warder do with Joseph? (v22)

What did Potiphar put Joseph in charge of? Solve the clues to find out

1st letter of ♥	
1st letter of 🐙	
2nd letter of (button)	
1st letter of (snowman)	
2nd letter of (pear)	
2nd letter of (sheep)	
2nd letter of (football)	
3rd letter of (igloo)	
4th letter of (ladder)	

MEMORY VERSE

"Those who honour me I will honour..."

1 Samuel ch 2 v 30

Draw Joseph running away from Potiphar's wife

The CUPBEARER and the BAKER

You can read this story in Genesis chapter 40

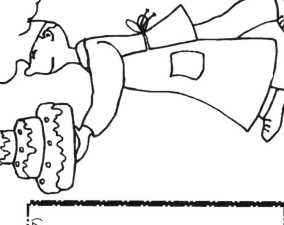

MEMORY VERSE

"Always be prepared to give an answer to everyone who asks you to give the reason for the hope that you have. But do this with gentleness and respect"

1 Peter chapter 3 verse 15

Draw what the baker dreamt (v 16 & 17)

Draw what the cupbearer dreamt (v 9 - 11)

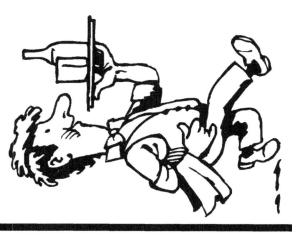

What did the cupbearer's dream mean? (verses 12 & 13)

What did the baker's dream mean? (verses 18 & 19)

PHARAOH'S DREAMS

You can read about Pharaoh's dreams in Genesis chapter 41

QUESTIONS............

By which river was Pharaoh standing in his dream? (v1)

What came out of the river first? (v2)

What came out of the river next? (v3)

What happened to the sleek, fat cows? (v4)

In Pharaoh's second dream, how many healthy ears of corn were growing? (v5)

What was the second lot of corn like? (v7)

Who did Pharaoh send for in the morning? (v8)

Who told Pharaoh about Joseph? (v9)

What did Pharaoh's dreams mean? (v29 and 30)

Why was the dream given to Pharaoh in two ways? (v32)

Who did Pharaoh put in charge of the palace? (v40)

What did Pharaoh put on Joseph? (v42)

What was the name of Joseph's wife? (v45)

How old was Joseph when he started working for Pharaoh? (v46)

What were the names of Joseph's two sons? (v51 and 52)

Draw Pharaoh asleep in bed

"Whoever gives heed (or pays attention) to instruction prospers, and blessed is he who trusts in the Lord"
Proverbs chapter 16 verse 20

Joseph's brothers go to Egypt

You can read this story in Genesis chapter 42

B	N	T	S	E	N	O	H	S	I	M	E	O	N	E
E	G	R	O	U	N	D	B	E	S	O	J	S	Y	G	N
S	N	O	S	C	J	O	K	O	M	H	A	P	E	Y	M	I
M	I	S	N	I	A	R	G	C	W	P	I	R	P	C	H	M
N	O	S	I	R	P	J	P	E	E	D	T	A	T	A	A
B	E	N	J	A	M	I	N	H	S	S	D	I	O	H	C	F
R	E	V	L	I	S	R	E	H	T	O	R	B	E	A	P	A
O	N	A	N	A	C	T	B	O	J	N	E	B	U	E	R

Find these words in the grid

Jacob
grain
Egypt
Joseph
ten
brothers
famine

Canaan
bowed
faces
ground
spies
honest
men
Pharaoh
Simeon

prison
silver
sack
Benjamin
Reuben
both
my
sons
die

How many words can you make from **FAMINE IN CANAAN** Write them on the back of this sheet

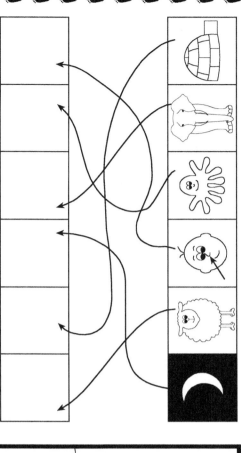

Take the first letter of each object & follow the arrows to find which brother was put in prison

EGYPT

MEMORY VERSE "Humble yourselves before the Lord, and He will lift you up" James chapter 4 verse 10

Joseph's brothers go to Egypt AGAIN!

You can read this story in Genesis chapter 43

Unjumble the words to find the memory verse:

"hTe sway fo het DROL rea grith;
eht grithsoue lawk ni meth,
tub eth lbeliorues tulsmbe ni meth"

"_ _ _ _ _ _ _ _ _ _ _ _ _ _ _ _ _ _ _ _;

_ _ _ _ _ _ _ _ _ _ _ _ _ _ _ _ , _ _ _

_ _ _ _ _ _ _ _ _ _ _ _ _ _ _ _ _ _"

Hosea ch 14 v 9

QUESTIONS!

Who was willing to guarantee Benjamin's safety? (v8 & 9)

What 6 gifts did they take to Egypt? (v11)

How much silver did Israel tell the brothers to take with them to Egypt? (v12)

What instructions did Joseph give to his steward when his brothers arrived? (v16)

What did Joseph say to Benjamin when he saw him? (v29)

How many times bigger was Benjamin's dinner than the rest of his brothers? (v34)

Draw the brothers eating with Joseph

A SILVER CUP

You can read this story in Genesis chapters 44 and 45

Draw Joseph crying as he tells his brothers who he is

Match the questions to the answers:

1. Whose sack was the silver cup in? (ch24 v12)

2. Who pleaded with Joseph? (ch24 v18)

3. Who told the steward to put the cup in a sack? (ch24 v2)

4. Where were Joseph's family going to live? (ch25 v10)

5. Where was Jacob living? (ch25 v 25)

A. Judah

B. Goshen

C. Canaan

D. Benjamin

E. Joseph

Memory Verse

"God sent me ahead of you to preserve for you a remnant on earth (or to make sure you have descendants) and to save your lives by a great deliverance" Genesis ch 45 v 7

Joseph said this, Who else in the Bible saved lives by a great deliverance? Look up 1 Timothy ch 1 v 15 in a Bible & write it here:

Joseph Judah Simeon Benjamin Reuben Egypt Jacob Corn Famine

Find these words in the sack:

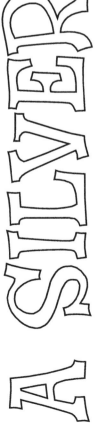

J	C	A	C	J	A	C	O	B
C	O	P	U	C	D	R	B	E
A	R	S	I	L	V	E	R	N
N	N	I	E	E	F	E	E	J
A	E	M	B	P	U	G	V	A
A	N	E	J	B	H	Y	E	M
N	I	O	E	S	A	P	A	I
J	M	N	A	S	D	T	L	N
S	A	C	K	A	U	A	E	O
S	F	O	O	D	J	C	D	O

Silver Cup Sack Food Canaan Revealed

Jacob goes to Egypt

You can read this story in Genesis Chapters 46 & 47

Answer the questions to find out how many years Jacob lived in Egypt
All the answers can be found in chapter 47

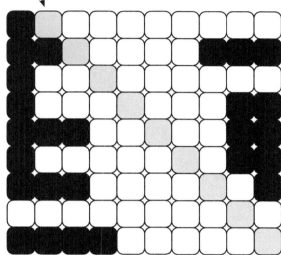

What did the brothers do for a job? (v3)

Where did Jacob NOT want to be buried? (v29)

What did the Egyptian give in exchange for food? (v16)

In which district did Joseph's family settle? (v11)

What was used up? (v15)

Whose land DIDN'T Joseph buy? (v22)

What was Jacobs other name? (v29)

Who settled in Goshen? (v27)

In which region did the Israelites settle? (v27)

Joseph's entire family was coming from Canaan. Use your Bible to fill in the names of Jacob's grandsons (ch46)

Reuben had 4 sons

Simeon had 6 sons

Levi had 3 sons

Judah had 5 sons

Issacher had 4 sons

Zebulun had 3 sons

Gad had 7 sons

Asher had 4 sons

Benjamin had 10 sons

Dan had 1 son

Naphtali had 4 sons

Crack the code to find the Memory Verse

▲	□	○	✿	☾	✚	♀	╱	△	◇	●	◖	✛	★	)	Ⴑ	ⵡ	Ⲱ	■	▽
A	B	C	D	E	F	H	I	L	M	N	O	P	R	S	T	U	W	Y	Z

" ◖★ ☾◇☾◇ □◖★   ■◖◖★   ○★◖▲Ⴑ◖★

_____   _____

╱○● Ⴑ♀☾ ✿▲■) ◖✛ ■◖◖★

___ ___ _____ __ _____

■◖ⵡ♀ „   ☾○○△◖)▽╱▲)Ⴑ◖)

_____ . _____

Ch 12 v 1

→ **All those boys! Imagine the party when they all arrived in Egypt with all the women, children, servants & animals too! What sort of things do you think they would have been talking about? Write them here:**

How do you think Jacob felt when he saw Joseph for the first time in about 20 years?

You can read this story in Genesis chapters 48 - 50

MEMORY VERSE

My thoughts are not your thoughts, neither are your ways My ways, declares the Lord

Isaiah ch 55 v 8

What did an angel deliver Jacob from? Solve the puzzle to find out

2nd letter of 🐑	2nd letter of	4th letter of 💗	2nd letter of ☂

Angel
Head
Right
Hand
Left
Die
Sword
See
Age
Put
No
Get

Fill in the numbers using your Bible:

Jacob had ☐ sons

Jacob had ☐ daughter

Jacob lived in Egypt for ☐ years

Jacob died when he was ☐ years old

The physicians took ☐ days to embalm Jacob

The Egyptians mourned for Jacob for ☐ days

Joseph died when he was ☐ years old

Dad
Too
God
Almighty
Fruitful
Increase
Descendants
Sons
Egypt
Men
Territory
Paddan
Knees
Ephrath
Isaac
Kissed
Arms
Bow
Gad
Take

Ephraim
Ill
Reuben
Jacob
Joseph
Simeon
Bed
Manasseh
Israel
Luz
Inherit
Canaan

E	S	A	E	R	C	N	I	M
J	N	R	I	G	H	T	N	A
A	O	A	N	A	B	A	A	N
C	E	S	H	R	G	K	A	A
O	M	C	E	A	M	E	N	S
B	I	A	R	P	N	I	A	S
A	S	A	I	A	H	D	C	E
L	M	S	T	S	N	O	S	H
M	K	I	S	S	E	D	T	H
I	S	R	A	E	L	F	N	E
G	E	T	L	R	E	T	A	G
H	P	T	U	L	H	U	D	Y	H	N	O
T	H	O	F	L	D	P	N	P	E	E	A
Y	R	O	T	I	R	R	E	T	A	B	L
D	A	D	I	B	O	S	C	S	D	U	E
O	T	A	U	O	W	E	S	B	M	E	G
G	H	G	R	W	S	E	E	N	K	R	N
L	U	Z	F	N	A	D	D	A	P	M	A

Find these words in the grid and with the letters left, unjumble them to find a famous Bible character →

Printed in Great Britain
by Amazon